Carnivorous Plants

NATURE'S PREDATORS

Kim T. Griswell

**KIDHAVEN
PRESS**™

San Diego • Detroit • New York • San Francisco • Cleveland
New Haven, Conn. • Waterville, Maine • London • Munich

For more information, contact
KidHaven Press
27500 Drake Rd.
Farmington Hills, MI 48331-3535
Or you can visit our Internet site at http://www.gale.com

LIBRARY OF CONGRESS CATALOGING-IN-PUBLICATION DATA

Griswell, Kim T.
  Carnivorous plants / by Kim T. Griswell
    p. cm. — (Nature's predators)
  Includes bibliographical references (p.   ).
  Summary: Discusses meat-eating plants, their life cycles, how they lure their prey, where different species are located, and what is being done to protect endangered carnivorous plants and their habitats.
    ISBN 0-7377-1387-9 (hardback : alk. paper)
  1. Carnivorous plants—Juvenile literature. [1. Carnivorous plants.] I. Title. II. Series.
  QK917 .G75 2003
  593'.75—dc21

                                        2001004875

Contents

Chapter 1

Silent Predators

In tropical rain forests, along coastal plains, and atop snowy mountains, strange life-forms silently wait for victims. Nearly six hundred species of this natural **predator** live all over the world. Few would suspect, by looking at them, that they are waiting to ambush their next meal. Why not? Because these hungry hunters are not animals. They are plants.

All plants make their own food through **photosynthesis**. They use the sun's energy to turn water and carbon dioxide into glucose, a kind of sugar. But some are not satisfied by nutrients taken from the soil, air, and water. These plants have an appetite for a different kind of meal. They are **carnivorous** plants, meat eaters.

Plants that eat animals lie in wait on every continent on Earth except Antarctica. These silent predators grow in every climate from tropical to arctic, wet to dry. The tall, leafy pitcher plant grows from the low wetlands of North America to the high mountains of Venezuela. The sticky sundew grows in fiery Australia, but it also lurks in frigid Siberia.

The most familiar carnivorous plant, the Venus flytrap, has a much smaller **habitat**. It grows only along the coastal plain of southeastern North Carolina and extreme northeastern South Carolina. It usually grows in wet meadowlands called savannas. The Venus flytrap can also be found in damp, sandy, peaty soils on the edges of swamps and bogs.

Bladderworts are the most adaptable meat-eating plants. They survive in a variety of habitats from the tropics to the Arctic. They can live in water, on land, or in trees. They can even hide out inside other plants, such as bromeliads, just waiting for a meal to come their way.

Carnivore Country

Carnivorous plants cluster together in colonies or grow scattered throughout a habitat. Different species of carnivorous plants often share the same hunting grounds. As many as thirteen species might be found in a single bog. In North Carolina, Venus flytraps, pitcher plants, and sundews can be found living together. In Oregon, sundews can be found with cobra plants. In Venezuela, sun pitchers and sundews share the high mountains.

Though carnivorous plants live around the world, more kinds grow in North America than anywhere

Carnivorous Plant Territory

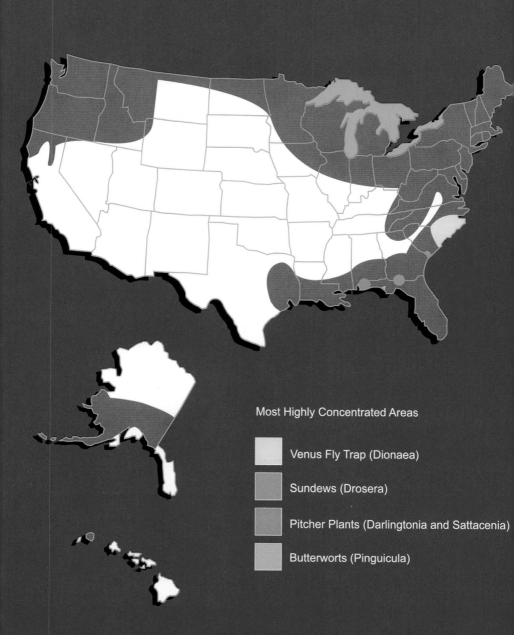

Most Highly Concentrated Areas

Venus Fly Trap (Dionaea)

Sundews (Drosera)

Pitcher Plants (Darlingtonia and Sattacenia)

Butterworts (Pinguicula)

else. Meat-eating plants grow in Canada and in every one of the fifty United States. Yet, one area might be called "carnivore country." Almost 90 percent of North America's killer plants lie low along a crescent that stretches from Virginia to Texas.

Much of carnivore country lies along the Atlantic and Gulf coastal plains. The damp savannas and wet bogs in this area provide ideal habitats for these hungry hunters.

Hungry, Hungry Plants

Though meat-eating plants live in so many places, their habitats share one characteristic: water. Almost all carnivorous plants grow in wet, poorly drained soil such as swamps and bogs. They grow close to rivers and oceans, as well as in ditches along roadways. Like all plants, carnivorous plants make food from water and carbon dioxide and get nutrients from the soil. One of the most important nutrients is nitrogen. Plants need nitrogen to be healthy and to reproduce, but water in the soil can wash it away. That turns plants into hungry predators.

To survive, carnivorous plants must find other sources of nitrogen. They do not have to look far. Small nitrogen-rich sources creep, crawl, and fly by all the time. Most of the victims of carnivorous plants are insects. Hundreds of different kinds of insects have been found trapped inside these crafty predators. Flies, moths, ants, wasps, mosquitoes, and beetles are among their favorite treats.

Since these Venus flytraps soak in the shallow waters of a swamp, some of the nutrients they need to grow get washed away.

Perfect Prey

The kind of insect trapped often depends on the size of a plant's traps. Some bladderworts capture microscopic **paramecia** in their pinhead-sized traps. Pygmy sundews the size of pennies catch gnat-sized insects. The two-inch long traps of the Venus flytrap often snap shut over large ants. The two- to three-foot-tall traps of the yellow trumpet plant swallow flies, wasps, beetles, and moths.

Larger animals also fall prey to these deadly killers. Cobra plants with leaves up to three feet

This gecko could not escape the firm grasp of a Venus flytrap.

long can trap and kill Pacific tree frogs. Giant hanging pitcher plants that grow in India and Borneo are even large enough to drown rats and birds. Spiders, slugs, worms, tadpoles, frogs, and lizards have all been trapped and eaten by hungry plants.

Bug Soup

Once carnivorous plants capture their insect victims, digestive juices go to work turning them into meals. Almost all carnivorous plants have special glands to aid digestion. These glands secrete **enzymes** that cover the captured prey. The enzymes dissolve the prey the same way an animal's stomach digests meat. In many carnivorous plants, bacteria help the enzymes break down the animal tissue, just as they do in the soil or in the air. But

An ant and a grasshopper drown in a pitcher plant's digestive enzymes.

some plants rely solely on bacterial action to digest their prey. These digestive juices are weak, like saliva, so they cannot hurt humans. But they are strong enough to turn small animals such as ants,

The hairlike follicles of the sundew plant release sticky juices that surround its prey.

spiders, and tadpoles, into a juicy soup. Once the prey is turned into soup, this liquid food is absorbed through the cell walls of the plant's leaves.

When the meal is finished, nothing remains of the victim but its hard, outer husk. Until wind and rain remove these remains, the dead insect bodies warn other insects that this pretty plant is not as friendly as it looks. Most carnivorous plants get ready for their next meal by resetting their traps. Those with snap traps, such as Venus flytraps and bladderworts, reopen. Those with tentacles, such as sundews, unfold. Those with jug traps, such as pitcher plants, always have their mouths open, ready for their next victim.

Chapter 2

Plants That Move

Plants cannot chase down prey the way animals do, so how do they capture their meals? Strangely enough, with their leaves! The two main types of leaf traps are active and passive. Like something out of a scary movie, plants with active traps have parts that can move to capture and enclose their prey.

The Nightmare Plant

When most people think of carnivorous plants, they picture the Venus flytrap with its open red jaws hungry for a meal. The plant grows from a short, thick **rhizome**, or underground stem. It produces a rosette, or rose-shaped pattern, of leaves. Each leaf has two parts: the **petiole**, or leaf base, and the true leaf at the end of the petiole. The heart-shaped petiole may hug the ground or stretch several inches into the air. The true leaf

After the clenching jaws of a Venus flytrap digest its prey, the insect's hard, outer shell is all that remains.

looks much like a small bear trap at the end of the petiole. A healthy Venus flytrap may have between six and fifteen traps clustered around the plant.

The open trap looks and smells inviting. The upper surface of the leaf is covered with tiny red or purple glands. Glands along the rim secrete **nectar**. The bright color and sweet nectar lure insects hoping for a free meal. But this meal will probably be their last.

The Trigger Hairs

On the inside of either open leaf are three tiny trigger hairs. The moment an insect brushes against any of the hairs, snap! The trap closes instantly and the insect is trapped.

Along the edge of the leaf trap are spines, called cilia, that lock together like the fingers of two hands. When the trap first closes, small insects, such as gnats and fruit flies, can crawl out between these fingers and escape. The plant seems to know that it takes more energy to digest these tiny insects than would be gained by eating them. But a larger insect, such as a fly, a moth, or a beetle, is not so lucky. Not only can it not get out, as it struggles inside the closed trap it also keeps touching the trigger hairs. This causes the trap to squeeze tighter and tighter, sealing the fate of its prey.

A Tiny, Efficient Killer

Being small does not stop a carnivorous plant from being deadly. An entire bladderwort may be only a

Venus Flytrap Anatomy

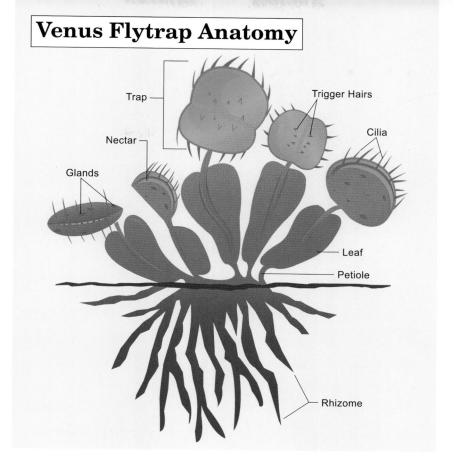

Trap

Nectar

Glands

Trigger Hairs

Cilia

Leaf

Petiole

Rhizome

few inches across, though some grow up to several yards long. Lying in wait, these rootless plants look something like green slime. Their stems creep underground or float in water like long, thin hairs. Kidney-, pear-, or tube-shaped bladders attach to the stems by small stalks. Hundreds to thousands of bladders scatter along the stems. Though the clear bladders look like they help the plant float, they are actually deadly traps.

When set, the bladder's walls curve inward to create a strong vacuum. Long hairs guide unwary prey toward a small door at one end of the bladder. Like the Venus flytrap, the bladderwort is set off by

The bladderwort uses its bulb-shaped traps to suck up unsuspecting victims.

trigger hairs. The tiniest touch sets off the trigger hairs and the door swings open. As the vacuum releases, the victim and the water around it are sucked inside. The prey is drawn into the trap in as little as fifteen-thousandths of a second. The trap door slams shut. Within minutes, the water is pumped out. The bladder seals and the plant begins to digest the creature.

Though death by digestion is tough on any creature, the bladderwort has a truly gruesome death in store for bigger prey. Tadpoles and mosquito **larvae** are too big to be sucked inside, so the bladderwort catches them by their tails. The trap digests the tail first. As the prey struggles to get free, it sets off the trap again. The trap reopens and sucks in another bite. As it is digested, the prey continues to struggle. The trap continues to reopen. Each time, a bit more of the prey is sucked inside. Bite by bite, the trap consumes and digests its prey. In the end, nothing is left but the head, which is too large to fit through the trap door.

Killer Tentacles

Like the Venus flytrap and the bladderwort, sundews have active traps. Their sticky leaves curl around their prey. Sundew leaves come in many shapes, including round, pear, and spoon shapes. Some have leaves that are long and thin like blades of grass. Others have leaves that branch out like a fern. Dozens of tiny, sticky hairs known as tentacles sprout from each leaf. At the tip of

Fooled by the sweet smell of the sundew plant's gooey nectar, a beetle cannot escape the plant's sticky grasp.

each tentacle is a small, brightly colored gland. Each gland secretes a shiny substance that makes the delicate leaves glisten with what looks like dew.

The glands on the ends of a sundew's tentacles have a deadly purpose. They secrete substances that help them lure, capture, and kill their next meal. A sweet nectar lures the prey. Insects follow the smell to the leaves, ready for a sugary treat. But the sundew has a trick in store. The shining stuff that looks like dew is really more like glue.

One touch of an insect's leg or wing and it finds itself stuck fast to the sundew's killer tentacles.

As the sundew goes into action, its tentacles begin to move. The edges of the leaves curl inward, wrapping around the struggling insect. It usually takes about twenty minutes for a sundew's tentacles to wrap up a meal, but it can take up to twenty-four hours. As the leaf wraps tighter, the glue may cover the breathing holes on the insect's abdomen. The insect suffocates. If not killed by suffocation, the insect will continue to struggle. It may tear off its own legs or wings trying to get away, but few escape.

The writhing follicles of the sundew plant wrap themselves around the legs of this damselfly.

The Greediest Plants

Though plants such as the Venus flytrap can snap shut in less than a second, they catch only one victim at a time. Flypaper traps such as sundews are far greedier predators. A hundred tiny insects might be caught on a single fifteen-inch-tall plant. A two-acre stand of sundews once captured as many as 6 million migrating butterflies. For their size, sundews can capture more insects than other carnivorous plants, making them the deadliest plant predator.

Chapter 3

The Deadly
Pit

Plants with passive traps do not move. They do not need to. These crafty predators get their victims to come to them. Pitcher plants are the most plentiful passive trappers. Their leaves form hollow vessels which capture prey. There are many different species of pitchers. Each one uses some mix of sweet nectar, bright colors, and glowing windows to lure prey into their poisonous pits.

Poison Parrots and Deadly Cobras

Many North American pitcher plants come from two families: Sarracenia and Darlingtonia. The structure, shape, and color of pitchers vary greatly from genus to genus. Many have names that describe how they look.

Plants in the Sarracenia family look like trumpets or skinny pitchers with lids. They either lie

The sweet scent of the trumpet plant entices prey down a long, perilous path.

along the ground or stand upright. Parrot pitchers have four- to eight-inch tubelike leaves that lie in a rosette pattern along the ground. Each leaf ends in a hollow, puffed hood. The tip of the hood curls back toward the center of the plant and ends in a pointed beak. This beak gives the parrot pitcher its name.

The yellow trumpet plant gets its name from its long, bright yellow hanging flowers. The sweet trumpet is named for the scent of its small, red flowers. They can smell like roses or cherry Kool-Aid. The hooded pitcher plant gets its name from its domed hood. This hood makes the top of the leaf look like an open, grinning mouth.

The Darlingtonia family has only one member: the cobra plant. The leaves of this plant look like a cobra about to strike. They have rounded, flared hoods and red, forked fangs. Just beneath the

Like a snake poised to strike, the cobra plant awaits its next meal.

fangs is the cobra's mouth. As in all pitcher plants, this mouth provides an opening into the deadly tube. Once inside, few victims manage to find their way back out.

The Treacherous Trail

Heavy red veins run up the leaves of many pitchers. They act like paths leading prey to the most dangerous parts of the leaf. The narrow seam where the leaf comes together also acts as a trail. These pathways are baited by nectar glands. Following the scent of nectar, prey wanders toward the plant's open mouth.

The closer the insect gets to the pitcher's opening, the more nectar it will find. Around the mouth is a curled-in rim called a **nectar roll**. This part of the plant is extra sweet to entice insects inside. The back of the mouth where the lid joins the leaf also has many nectar glands. The heaviest nectar in a cobra plant is at the point where the fangs attach to the open mouth.

A pitcher plant's nectar does more than lead insects into its trap. It contains a drug that makes the insect unsteady, as if drunk. Unsteady insects wobble right into the plant's open mouth. If insects drink enough nectar, they can become paralyzed or even die.

False Windows

Besides sweet trails that lead insects into trouble, pitchers may also have "windows" to trick their

The red veins of the pitcher plant lead insects to its mouthlike trap.

prey. The hooded pitcher plant, the cobra plant, and the parrot pitcher all share this insect lure. They have **translucent** areas that allow light to enter the pitcher. Sun glows through these areas, inviting insects to come inside.

Flying insects that land on the pitcher's rim may see these windows as escape hatches. When insects fly toward these false openings, they slam into the leaf. Stunned, they fall into the digestive juices below.

Crawling insects feeding on the rim may also head toward these windows. Once they leave the rim to reach the windows, they run into another problem. Downward pointed hairs in this area keep them from crawling or flying back out. They can only go down, straight toward the deadly pit.

A Slippery Slope

Once victims wander into the interior of the pitcher, they are in trouble. Just inside the pitcher's open mouth, the leaf is as slippery as a waxed slide. When victims step on this waxy surface, they slip right into the pitcher's trap. As the pitcher narrows, the prey may try to fly or climb back out. Either way there is little chance of escape. The beat of an insect's wings creates a vacuum that sucks it farther down. Toward the bottom of the trap, hairs grow pointing downward. Like sharp needles, these hairs keep insects from escaping.

Glands line the slippery walls inside the trap. These do not secrete sweet nectar like those on the

A roach tastes the pitcher plant's sweet nectar, then
climbs into its deadly tube searching for more.

outside of the leaf and at its mouth. They drip digestive juices. These juices collect at the bottom of the tube. As insects fill the trap, the plant produces more liquid, dissolving its prey to feed its hunger.

Big-Bellied Predators

The strangest, most frightening pitcher plants come from the Nepenthe family. These tropical plants grow stems that climb through trees or run along the ground. Long, flat leaves grow from these viney stems. A single tendril shoots out from the end of each leaf. A loop forms on the tendril, then swings upright. The end of the tendril swells into a pitcher. Depending on the species, the pitchers vary in color from cream to green to shades of red. They may have white, violet, brown, or crimson spots. At first, the pitcher's lid remains closed. As the pitcher matures, the lid pops open. Once the lid opens up, the plant is ready to lure, capture, and kill its prey.

Because tropical pitchers can be up to eighteen inches tall and hold several quarts of digestive fluid, they can capture bigger prey than other pitcher plants. Birds, rats, and other small animals have fallen into their gaping mouths. Though these bigger victims drown, no one knows for certain whether the plants can dissolve and digest such large prey.

Bigger victims are not all that sets tropical pitchers apart. Some also look more deadly than their North American counterparts. The most dan-

The big-bellied pitcher plant is large enough to capture rats, birds, and other small animals.

gerous looking tropical pitcher has a row of long, curved hooks all the way around its lip. These hooks are as sharp as knives. Another pitcher has two hard, sharp fangs that grow beneath its lid. Nectar sometimes drips like venom from these fangs. The slippery fangs lead ants and other insects to their death, but they may also keep small animals from raiding their traps. In fact, the remains of small animals have been found caught in these deadly fangs.

Chapter 4

Preying on Plants

Carnivorous plant traps die naturally through-out the life of the plant. During their active growth cycle, Venus flytraps and sundews continually replace older leaves with new ones. Pitcher plant leaves are in their prime for up to a few months. Many carnivorous plants become dormant in winter or during times of drought. Their leaves die back and the plants rest.

The normal life cycle is not the only thing that kills the traps of carnivorous plants. Trapping too much prey or capturing prey that is too large to digest can also kill a leaf trap. And sometimes, these crafty predators become prey.

Plant Pirates

As the hollow leaves of pitcher plants fill with prey, insects and other animal pirates come looking for a free meal. Several kinds of spiders steal insect meals. Tree frogs cling to the mouths of some pitcher plants. They slurp up insects about to fall into the trap. Snails and slugs may also come by to snatch a snack.

Red crab spiders rob tropical pitchers. The spider attaches itself to the inside of the trap by a small thread. Swinging on this thread, it snatches flies that fall into the trap. The spider can even fish mosquito larvae from the digestive fluid. If threatened, the spider plunges right into the plant's deadly soup. Once the danger passes, it pulls itself out using its silky lifeline. Some ants can also dive

---

Camouflaged on the rim of a pitcher plant, a green tree frog looks to steal an insect meal.

safely into the pitcher's pool. They pull out larger insects, such as cockroaches. Then they tear the insects apart, eating what they like and throwing the rest back into the soup.

Bigger animals also take advantage of carnivorous plants. A small insect-eating primate called a tarsier lives on the island of Borneo. It visits tropical pitchers to pirate fresh prey. Birds also visit the plants, scavenging insect larvae that live inside. Though it may seem that stealing the plant's food would hurt, some think it actually helps. Too many insects in a pitcher can lead to its death.

Home, Deadly Home

More than 150 creatures make pitcher plants their homes or benefit in some way from the plants. The pitchers' hollow leaves provide moisture, shade, and a supply of trapped prey. Sixteen species of insects or other small creatures live nowhere else but inside North American pitcher plants.

Mites, and mosquito and fly larvae live unharmed in the pitchers' digestive juices. They swim through the deadly soup, feasting upon the pitcher plant's prey. Though they steal their meals, these tiny pirates seem to be helping their hosts. As they feed, they break down larger prey into nutrients the plant can use.

Toxic Nurseries

Insects that live inside pitcher plants are not always helpful. The Exyra moth lays its eggs on the inner wall of the pitcher leaf. The moth's larvae hatch inside and feed upon the leaf's tissue as they grow. To keep itself safe, the moth closes the mouth of the pitcher. It can chew a groove around the inside of the pitcher. This causes the leaf to wilt and

A tarsier has a tasty meal after snatching a cicada from a pitcher plant.

A curious wolf spider finds itself glued to the sticky tentacles of a sundew plant.

seals the opening. The moth can also spin a web to close the pitcher's mouth. With its mouth closed, the pitcher can no longer capture prey to feed itself.

The Sarracenia wasp turns pitcher plants into a nursery. First, the wasp stuffs the lower pitcher with grass or moss. Next, it adds a layer of dead grasshoppers or crickets. The wasp lays its eggs among the dead insects. It fills the leaf with layers of grass and insects, sealing the top with a final layer of grass. When its eggs hatch, the larvae dine on the dead insects. A leaf thus filled can no longer feed the pitcher plant.

The Deadliest Foe

Though carnivorous plants can capture and kill all kinds of prey, they cannot bite back against their deadliest foe: humans. All over the world, the natural habitats of meat-eating plants have been destroyed. In the United States, wetlands filled with Venus flytraps and pitcher plants have been drained. People build homes and malls on the dried-out land. In Europe, moors once filled with sundews have been poisoned by agricultural runoff. In Asia, people slash and burn the habitats of tropical pitcher plants to make farms. In Australia, golf courses have replaced pitcher plant habitats.

Draining, poisoning, or clearing wetlands is not the only danger to carnivorous plants. When trees and plants invade bogs, they crowd out carnivorous plants. Natural fires started by lightning once kept out these invaders. In the 1930s the U.S. Forest

Service wanted to protect nearby towns and timber. They decided to stop the fires. With no fires to clear the bogs, carnivorous plants had little room to grow.

Plant poachers are also a danger. Rare tropical pitchers can sell for hundreds of dollars. Poachers take whole plants from the wild to sell to collectors. Commercial suppliers also raid fields for plants because stealing plants is cheaper than growing them. People who want carnivorous plants in their gardens also remove whole plants from the wild. Collectors need permits to take pitcher plants from the wild, but each year millions of leaves are harvested illegally.

Protecting Plant Predators

Plants that lurk and lure are not only natural predators, but also natural wonders. Governments and conservation groups are working to protect them for future generations.

A game warden takes off after a plant poacher who has just stolen a Venus flytrap from a reserve.

A cluster of trumpet plants stands within view of a game warden as he surveys the area.

The United States protects pitcher plants and other meat eaters. North Carolina levies fines of up to $2,000 for taking a Venus flytrap without a permit. Mexico protects butterworts, a sticky trapper similar to the sundew. Trying to smuggle a tropical pitcher plant from Borneo can land a plant collector in jail for two years. In the United States a nonprofit group called The Nature Conservancy buys and manages endangered habitats. Across the world The International Carnivorous Plant Society works to protect endangered plants and their wetland homes. These efforts will help ensure that these silent, hungry predators can continue to hunt in wetlands all over the world.

Glossary

carnivorous: Feeding on meat.

enzyme: A complex substance made by living cells.

habitat: The place where a plant or animal naturally lives and grows.

larvae: The wormlike forms that hatch from the eggs of insects.

nectar: A sweet liquid produced by many plants.

nectar roll: The curled-in rim of a pitcher plant leaf, coated with sweet liquid produced by the plant.

paramecia: Tiny, one-celled organisms shaped like ovals or slippers.

petiole: A slender stem that supports a leaf.

photosynthesis: The process by which plants use sunlight, water, and carbon dioxide to make food.

predator: A creature that lives by preying on other organisms.

rhizome: A thick underground stem.

translucent: Letting some light through.

For Further Exploration

Books

Mary Batten, *Hungry Plants*. New York: Golden Books, 2000. This book explains why some plants bait, snap, trick, and trap insects. Includes information on how carnivorous plants have been used to cure sickness.

Tony Camilleri, *Carnivorous Plants*. Sydney, Australia, Kangaroo Press, 1998. Big, color photographs give close-up views of meat-eating plants. Maps show each plant's natural habitat. Shows how to plant and care for a carnivorous home garden.

Nancy J. Nielsen, *Carnivorous Plants*. New York: Franklin Watts, 1992. Learn more about meat-eating plants such as waterwheels, butterworts, and pitcher plants. Then discover how to grow them at home or in your backyard.

Richard Platt, *Plants Bite Back!* New York: DK Publishing, 1999. Part of the Eyewitness Readers series, this book begins with meat eaters and moves on to plants that sting, burn, and produce poisons. Includes lots of colorful illustrations and photographs.

Website

The Carnivorous Plant FAQ (www.sarracenia. com). Dr. Barry Meyers-Rice finds answers to all kinds of questions about carnivorous plants. This carnivorous plant expert answers common questions simply and with humor. Includes fun animations that show plants eating insects.

Index

Picture Credits

About the Author

Author Kim T. Griswell has written hundreds of short stories and articles for children, as well as educational materials for elementary grade teachers. She loves to write about strange and interesting topics such as poison dart frogs, the aurora borealis, and UFOs. She has been a senior editor, a book development manager, and a university instructor. She is currently the coordinating editor of a children's magazine in Honesdale, Pennsylvania.